ITALY

Patricia Borlenghi and Rachel Wright

W
FRANKLIN WATTS
LONDON•SYDNEY

This symbol appears on some pages throughout this book. It indicates that adult supervision is advisable for that activity.

This edition 2007

Franklin Watts
338 Euston Road
London NW1 3BH

Franklin Watts Australia
Hachette Children's Books
Level 17/207 Kent Street
Sydney, NSW 2000

© Franklin Watts 1994, 2003

Editor: Hazel Poole
Consultant: Fabiana Ramella
Designer: Sally Boothroyd
Commissioned photography: Peter Millard
Artwork: John Shackell
Picture research: Ambreen Husain

A CIP catalogue record for this book is available from the British Library.

ISBN-13: 978 0 7496 7335 2

Printed in China

Franklin Watts is a division of Hachette Children's Books.

CONTENTS

Introducing Italy	4
Around Italy	6
Mini Mosaics	9
Shopping and Eating	10
A Passion for Pizza	12
Life in Italy	14
Industry and Technology	16
Tourism, Sport and Leisure	18
The Arts	20
Holidays and Festivals	23
Mystery Masks	26
Italian History	28
Picture Pairs	30
Index	32

Introducing Italy

*B*envenuti in Italia!
Welcome to Italy!
Before you start to explore,
here are a few useful facts
about the country.

FLYING THE FLAG

*T*he Italian flag, *la
bandiera tricolore*, has
green, white and red stripes
and was first used in 1797.
It is similar to the French
flag, but has a green stripe
instead of blue. Green is
the symbol of nature and
man's natural rights -
equality and liberty.

ITALY IN THE WORLD

*I*taly lies in Southern Europe and is a peninsular
surrounded by sea. It covers 301,245 square kilometres
and looks like a high-heeled boot with the island of Sicily
at its toe. Italy borders France, Switzerland, Austria and
Slovenia.

Italy, officially known as *la Repubblica Italiana*, was one
of the six founders of the European Economic Community
(EEC, now the European Union or EU). Italy has a
population of around 57.5 million people. The capital city
is *Roma* (Rome) - "the eternal city".

FRATELLI D'ITALIA

*T*he Italian
national anthem
is *Fratelli d'Italia*,
composed in 1847 by
Goffredo Mameli, a
patriot and poet. It
became the national
anthem in 1946.

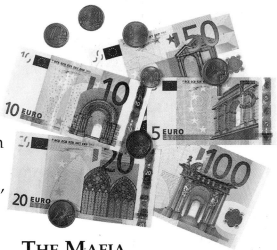

MONEY

The Italian currency is called the *euro*. It replaced the *lira* as the national currency in February 2002. Euros can be used to purchase goods in any of 12 European countries. The 'head' or national side of each coin has a different image on it, depending on which country it was made in. One euro is divided into 100 *cents*. You can get bank notes for the following amounts: 5, 10, 20, 50, 100, 200 and 500 euros. There are coins for 1 and 2 euros, as well as for 1, 2, 5, 10, 20 and 50 cents.

GOVERNMENT

The Head of State is the President, who is elected every seven years, but the Prime Minister runs the country. The parliament is made up of the Chamber of Deputies and the Senate, whose members are elected every five years. However, Italy's politics are beset by corruption and financial scandals.

CAR REGISTRATION

Italian car numbers are fun to identify. You can tell which city or town the car is from by looking at the number plate. For example, cars from Milan have MI on their number plate. The only place where the whole name is used is ROMA, for Rome.

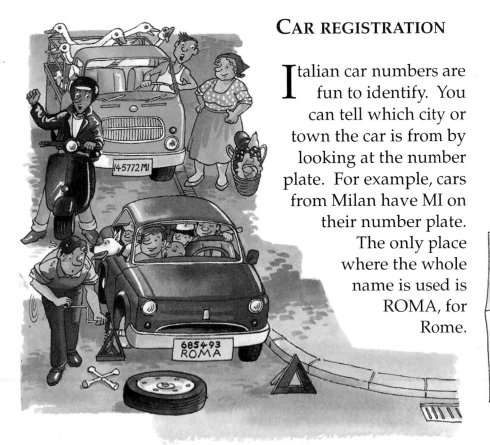

THE MAFIA

The Italian Mafia is an organised crime ring, which originated from Sicily. The *Mafiosi* (Mafia members) have interests in controlling many aspects of Italian life, including politics, business and the law. Most of their activities are illegal, such as international drug-smuggling and bribing officials. In recent times, many high-profile members of the Mafia have been caught and imprisoned in an attempt to weaken the influence of the organisation.

Say it in Italian
la bandiera - flag
il francobollo - stamp
i soldi - money
l'Italia - Italy
gli italiani - the Italians
la carta - map

Around Italy

Italy is divided into 20 regions and 95 provinces. A lot of the land is hilly and some of the mountains are volcanic. The Alps stretch along the north and on the east they become known as the Dolomites. The Apennines run down the middle of the country and are known as the "backbone" of Italy.

Italy's regions are divided into provinces and municipalities called *comuni*. Each of these has an elected council. The regions must abide by the laws of the national government but they are allowed to make local laws.

San Marino is a tiny independent republic in its own right and has its own flag. It is one of the oldest states in Europe.

The Vatican City is also a separate state occupying only 0.44 square kilometres. It has its own flag, currency and stamps and there are some areas that can only be entered with special permission. The Pope lives in the Vatican City.

DIALECTS

Italian is the official language. It is based on the Florentine dialect (from Florence). German and French are also spoken around the Italian borders, Each region has its own dialect, but there are many more variations. These have been influenced by French, German, Greek, Spanish, Arabic and Celtic words. Sicilian is spoken in Sicily and Sardinians have their own dialect called "Sardo".

CLIMATE

In Northern Italy, winters are cold and wet but the summers are hot and dry. This is a continental climate. In the south, winters are mild, springs are sunny and summers are very hot and dry. This is a Mediterranean climate. In the winter, there is snow in the mountains, even in the south of Italy. The peaks of the Alps are always covered in snow, both in winter and summer.

Average temperatures		
Place	**January**	**July**
Milan	5°C	29°C
Rome	11°C	30°C
Naples	12°C	29°C

ARCHITECTURE

Italy contains a wonderful variety of architecture. In Roman times, town planning was very sophisticated. The Romans invented concrete and were the first to use the arched vault. They continued the Greek tradition of mosaics by pressing tiny bits of stone into wet plaster. The Romans used uniform shapes and matching numbers of arches and columns. They had a great influence on Italian artists of the Renaissance.

Today lots of monuments are crumbling, but most of the old city centres are preserved as they were many years ago.

POMPEII

Pompeii was a Roman town near Naples. In AD 57 it was buried by lava and ash from Mount Vesuvius, a volcano near Naples. You can still visit the ruins and see what Roman houses, streets and shops used to look like.

THE COLISEUM

The Coliseum in Rome was used by the ancient Romans as an arena for sport and entertainment.

VOLCANOES

Italy is unique as it has two very famous and active volcanoes. The highest volcano in Europe is Mount Etna in Sicily which is 3,343 metres high. It still erupts today.

The Lipari (or Aeolian) islands include the volcano on Stromboli, which is still active. The beaches are full of black sand and pumice stone. Many islanders are scared of the volcano and call it "he".

THE LEANING TOWER OF PISA

This is one of Italy's most famous landmarks. It is the bell tower of Pisa cathedral, which was leaning so badly that it had to be closed to the public. It was reopened in 2001.

VENICE

The city of Venice is built on 118 small islands, joined together by 100 canals. There are nearly 400 bridges crossing the canals. St. Mark's Square and St. Mark's Church are famous landmarks of this city.

LA BASILICA DI SAN PIETRO

The Basilica, in the Vatican City, Rome, is built on the spot where St. Peter was buried. This is the world's largest church and is very ornate.

FLORENCE

Florence is a beautiful city situated on both sides of the River Arno. Cars are not allowed in many parts of the city centre. The *Duomo di Santa Maria del Fiore* is a main feature of this city.

Across the Arno is the famous *Ponte Vecchio* (Old Bridge) which houses lots of jewellery shops selling fine gold and silver.

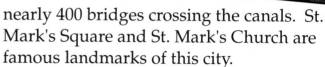

Say it in Italian
l'estate - summer
la primavera - spring
l'autunno - autumn
il tempo - weather
il sole - sun
la pioggia - rain
la montagna - mountain

Mini Mosaics

YOU WILL NEED:

eggshells, clear household varnish, pencil, 5 level tablespoons plaster of Paris, paint brushes, paper, poster paints, strip of white card, 40 cm X 2 cm, plasticine, rolling pin, knife, tweezers, sticky tape, empty jar, 5 tablespoons water

Keep a dry cloth beside you to wipe your fingers.

1. Wash the eggshells carefully. Let them dry and paint them. When the paint is dry, add a coat of varnish.

2. Roll out a slab of plasticine about 1/2 cm thick.

3. Fold the card into four and tape the ends together to make a square.

4. Press the card square firmly into the plasticine.

5. Draw a simple design for your mosaic.

6. Break the eggshells into pieces. Try not to make the pieces too small!

7. Put the plaster of Paris and water into the jar and stir well with the knife.

8. Pour the plaster into the card square. Using your design as a guide, carefully lay pieces of eggshell into the wet plaster. (Plaster of Paris dries quickly, so you will need to work fast). As the plaster hardens, gently press the eggshells into place with the tip of the tweezers. (If a piece of eggshell lands upside down, turn it over with the tweezers.)

9. When the plaster of Paris is nearly dry, peel away the card. When it is completely dry, remove the plasticine carefully.

9

Shopping and Eating

Italy produces 20 per cent of the world's wine, and there are vineyards in almost every region.

The Po Valley is the most important agricultural area in Italy, but there are small farms all over the country. Fruits such as oranges and lemons, peaches, apricots, plums and tomatoes are grown. Other important crops are wheat, maize, olives, rice, sugar beet, tobacco, potatoes, artichokes, garlic, onions, cauliflowers, beans, and flowers. Cattle, sheep, goats and pigs are reared on farms throughout the country, and fishing is widespread along the Italian coast.

Cheese is a major product of Italy. One of the most well-known is Parmesan cheese from Parma. Others include Mozzarella, made from buffalo milk, Bel Paese, Certosa, Fontina, and Mascarpone which is a cream cheese.

SHOPPING

There are now many supermarkets in Italy and also a few hypermarkets. However, many Italians like to buy fresh food daily, either from markets or small specialist shops.

Italian shops are usually open daily (except on Sundays) from 8.30 am to 12.30 pm and 3.30 pm to 7.30 pm. Banks in Italy are closed on Saturdays. They close one afternoon a week, but this varies regionally.

Shopping list
il pane - bread
il latte - milk
il formaggio - cheese
le uova - eggs
il tè - tea
le frutta - fruit
le verdure - vegetables
il pollo - chicken
il pesce - fish
il gelato - ice cream

Say it in Italian
il *supermercato* - supermarket
il *mercato* - market
il *panificio* - bakery
la *pasticceria* - cake shop
la *macelleria* - butcher's shop
alimentari - grocer's shop
la *gelateria* - ice cream shop
la *farmacia* - chemist
l'*ufficio postale* - post office
la *banca* - bank

EATING OUT

Italians love eating out, especially with their families. They often go to restaurants for Sunday lunch. *Trattorie* are smaller restaurants but good value, and *Tavole Calde* are cheap and serve hot food. *Rosticcerrie* serve take-away roasted meats and poultry. Street vendors sell everything from nuts and watermelons to pasta dishes.

Bars in Italy serve all kinds of drinks and sometimes brioche or croissants, panini (rolls), tramezzini (sandwiches) or tostati (toasted bread) They are open all day. Pizzerie (pizza parlours) are found all over Italy either for eating in or for take-away food.

PASTA

There are many varieties of pasta including spaghetti, tagliatelle, ravioli, penne, farfalle, ruote, paglia e fieno, vermicelli, tortelloni (big) and tortellini (small). Pasta is said to have been eaten in Etruscan times. It is usually served with a sauce or on its own with butter or olive oil, garlic and herbs.

In Italy there are regional differences in cooking, but there is usually a standard menu wherever you go.

Because Italy is almost an island, fish is a very important part of the menu. Sardines get their name from Sardinia, famous for its fish soup.

Italians eat a lot of fresh fruit, but on feast days they will prepare special desserts. Such a dessert is *Tiramisù* (pick-me-up) which is made from layers of sponge fingers dipped in black coffee and marsala, and mascarpone mixed with icing sugar. The top layer is sprinkled with chocolate powder. It is delicious.

MENU
Antipasto - hors d'oeuvres (usually includes a selection of cold meats including salami, coppa, bresaola, prosciutto, mortadella or vegetable/fish salads)
Lasagne al forno - baked lasagne
Spaghetti alla Bolognese - spaghetti with meat sauce, from Bologna
Calamari - squid
Petti di Pollo - chicken breasts
Parmigiana di Melanzane - baked aubergines
Zabaglione - egg punch

Ice cream is another great Italian invention, and there are hundreds of different varieties.

A Passion for Pizza

Pizza, as we know it, was invented in Naples during the 1700s. Sold from street stalls, it soon became popular with the Neapolitans and before long, *pizzerie* were set up in the city. News of this tasty tomato-topped dish spread quickly, and when Italy's Queen Margherita visited Naples in 1889, she insisted on trying a pizza for herself. Immediately three different pizzas were made for the Queen, one of which was topped with tomatoes, mozzarella cheese and basil. This was clearly the Queen's favourite and so it was named *Pizza Margherita*, in her honour.

To make four medium-sized Margherita pizzas.

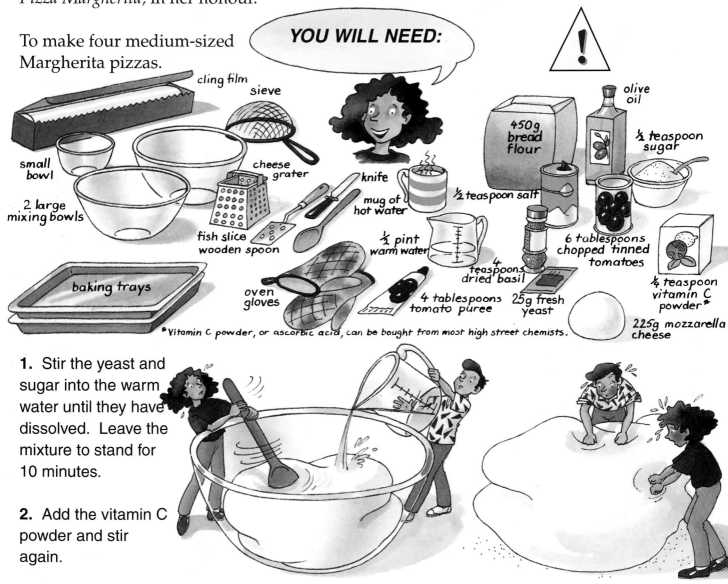

YOU WILL NEED:

cling film
sieve
olive oil
450g bread flour
½ teaspoon sugar
small bowl
cheese grater
knife
½ teaspoon salt
2 large mixing bowls
mug of hot water
fish slice
wooden spoon
½ pint warm water
4 teaspoons dried basil
6 tablespoons chopped tinned tomatoes
¼ teaspoon vitamin C powder*
baking trays
oven gloves
4 tablespoons tomato purée
25g fresh yeast
225g mozzarella cheese

*Vitamin C powder, or ascorbic acid, can be bought from most high street chemists.

1. Stir the yeast and sugar into the warm water until they have dissolved. Leave the mixture to stand for 10 minutes.

2. Add the vitamin C powder and stir again.

3. Tip the flour and salt into the mixing bowl. Add the yeast mixture and 3 tablespoons of olive oil. Mix everything together with the wooden spoon until you have a soft, springy ball of dough that leaves the sides of the bowl clean. If the dough is too sticky, add a little more flour. If it is too dry, add a little more oil.

4. Sprinkle some flour over your hands and work surface, and knead the dough with your hands.

5. Rub some oil around the inside of the second bowl. Put in the dough, cover it with cling film and leave it in a warm place for 15 minutes. (If the dough hasn't nearly doubled in size after 15 minutes, leave it a little longer.)

6. Preheat the oven to 425°F/220°C/gas mark 7. Lightly grease the baking trays with oil and, using oven gloves, put them in the oven.

7. When the dough has doubled in size, cut it into four. Dip your knife into the mug of hot water first, to stop the dough sticking to it.

8. Cover your work surface and hands with flour, and flatten and stretch each portion of dough into a round, about 20 cm across. Pinch the edges of each round with your fingers. This will stop the tomato topping dripping off the dough as it cooks.

9. Drain the tinned tomatoes well. Put them in the small bowl with the tomato puree and stir. Spread an equal amount of this mixture over each doughy base.

10. Grate the cheese and divide it between the four bases. Sprinkle a teaspoon of basil over each base and add a drop of olive oil.

11. Take the baking trays out of the oven. Transfer your pizzas to the trays and put them in the oven. Leave them to cook for 15-20 minutes and serve at once.

What do the Italian flag and a Margherita pizza have in common?

13

Life in Italy

HOUSING

Most Italians now live in apartments in cities or towns. Their homes are quite small, but usually have a *cantina* (cellar) for storing wine and other goods. People living in the suburbs generally own houses with gardens.

Northern Italy, with its crowded, polluted, traffic-filled cities enjoys a greater standard of living than the poorer, more agricultural southern region. The South is less advanced because of its lack of industry.

Family life is very important and families keep in regular contact. Italians often have second homes in the country areas where their families originally lived. They spend weekends there.

GOING TO SCHOOL

Children must go to school between the ages of 6-14. They attend *la scuola elementare* (primary school) until they are 11. There are two types of timetable - one for full time school, five days a week and one for six mornings and some afternoons only. After primary school, children attend *la scuola media inferiore* (junior secondary school) for three years. At the age of 14, children decide what subjects they wish to study at *la scuola media superiore* (senior secondary school). There are three kinds to choose from - *il liceo*, specialising in Classics, arts, languages or sciences; *la scuola tecnica*, technical school with courses in commerce, industry or agriculture; *l'istituto magistrale* for primary school teacher training qualification (although some go on to university).

After five years, students sit a national exam - *l'esame di stato* - in order to get into university. Italy has 59 universities in 36 cities.

RELIGION

Italy is predominantly a Roman Catholic country. Only one per cent of the population are Jewish, Protestant or Greek Orthodox. The Pope lives in the Vatican City in Rome and is the head of the Roman Catholic Church. People travel from all over the world to visit the Vatican.

Children make their first Holy Communion at the age of 7 - 10. Girls wear long white dresses and veils and boys wear suits.

At the age of 9 - 14, they are confirmed by a bishop. They also wear special or smart clothes on this occasion.

What People Do

Today more people work in industry than in agriculture. Others are employed in the wine and fishing industries. There are many public employees. In Italy, many forms are needed for even the simplest things - but it does keep people employed.

The Police Force

In Italy there are many different types of police. The *vigili urbani* (traffic police) wear white uniforms with white helmets and gloves in the summer, navy blue uniforms in the winter. They form part of the municipal police. The *Carabinieri* (Italian army corps) wear grey-green uniforms in the summer and black in the winter. They deal with crime and demonstrations.

The Media

Italy has more than 70 national daily newspapers. One of the most popular is *Il Corriere della Sera*, published in Milan. There are many weekly women's magazines including *Grazia, Marie Claire* and *Donna Moderna*. There are also news, topical and gossip magazines.

Italians love to watch television and officially there are 13 channels to choose from. There are three state-controlled channels but there are also over 100 independent or pirate stations.

Emergency telephone numbers
police 113
carabinieri 112
fire 114
road assistance and tourist advice 116

Say it in Italian:
l'insegnante - teacher
il medico - doctor
la scuola - school
la chiesa - church
il giornale - newspaper
il lavoro - work
la casa - house

Industry and Technology

INDUSTRY

Italy is the fourth biggest steel producer in Europe. Milan and Turin are the biggest industrial centres in Italy. The country is not rich in natural resources but has deposits of iron-ore, lead, zinc, aluminium and mercury. Italy has some coal and oil but most raw materials are imported. The hydro-electric industry - water being converted into electricity - is a major industry in the areas around the Alps. Italy is very rich in marble, and many homes have marble floors. The most famous marble is found at the Carrara quarries in Tuscany.

Sculptures are modelled from marble cut from the Carrara quarries in Tuscany.

TECHNOLOGY

Steel is necessary for Italy's car industry. Several well-known makes of car, such as Fiat, Alfa Romeo, Lancia, Lamborghini and Ferrari are made in Italy and exported all over the world.

Many household appliances, such as washing machines, dishwashers and refrigerators are made in Italy by companies like Zanussi.

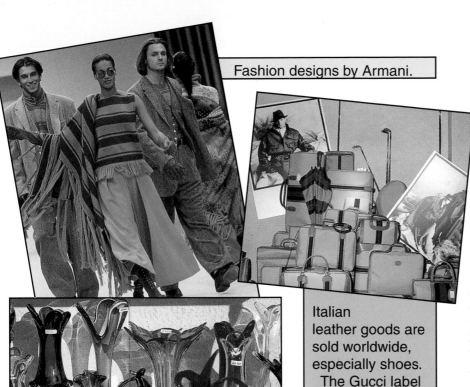

Fashion designs by Armani.

Italian leather goods are sold worldwide, especially shoes. The Gucci label stands for luxury.

Venetian glass is well-known for its ornamental designs.

FASHION AND DESIGN

Italians are renowned for design, both in clothing and home furnishing. The fashion and clothing industry is as important as tourism. Milan is famous for its *Collezioni* - the fashion collections. The greatest Italian fashion designers include Georgio Armani, Valentino, and Giovanni Versace. Italian design is very expensive and exclusive, but it is based on simple lines and elegance.

TRANSPORT

The public transport system is very well run. Rail fares are cheap and there are several different types of train from the IC (InterCity) train to *locale* (a slow local train stopping at every station).

Most cities and towns run cheap bus or tram services. The tickets are one price and can be bought from the *tabaccaio* or *edicola* (newsstand).

There is a huge motorway system (*autostrade*) which is the third largest in the world.

Italy's airports are smaller than other airports, but they are very busy and *Alitalia*, Italy's national airline, carries over 25 million people worldwide each year. In the summer months, you can fly direct to most of Italy's major tourist resorts.

Say it in Italian:
la macchina - car
il treno - train
l'autobus - bus
l'aereo - aeroplane
il viaggio - journey
il metro - tube

17

Tourism, Sport and Leisure

Italy is so beautiful and rich in culture that tourism is its most important industry, with hundreds of thousands of people visiting the country each year. There are many seaside resorts, but some have become polluted and crowded, especially on the Adriatic coast. The beaches there are popular because they are long and sandy. On the Mediterranean, the Ligurian coast is rocky and sheltered. The further south you go, the beaches become less crowded.

The islands of Capri and Ischia, near Naples, are very picturesque.

Here are just a few of the tourist spots in Italy:

SICILY

Sicilia has been influenced by many cultures and Siracusa is the birthplace of Archimedes. There are many interesting Greek temples to visit.

THE MOUNTAINS

The Alps and the Dolomites are excellent for skiing. Popular resorts are Courmayeur, near Mont Blanc, and Cortina d'Ampezzo. Italians also ski in the Appenines at weekends.

THE LAKES

The lakes south of the Alps are popular for holiday makers and for windsurfers. The most famous of these lakes are Como, Maggiore and Garda.

SPORT AND LEISURE

Although Italians love skiing, tobogganing and winter sports in general, the most popular sport is football. There are famous clubs such as Juventus, Inter, AC Milan and Lazio.

Rugby and golf are becoming increasingly popular and Italian rugby has now reached world class standard.

Cycling is another national favourite with the *Giro d'Italia* held in June. Car racing fans watch the Grand Prix at Monza, near Milan, or at Imola near Bologna.

Italians love to play card games and although they use conventional playing cards, they have a different set of cards from Naples. These have suits of swords (spades), cups (hearts), money (diamonds), and sticks (clubs).

Say it in Italian:
il calcio - football
la squadra - team
la partita - game
nuotare - to swim
fare vela - to sail
fare una partita a carte -
   to play cards

Italy has, over many centuries, created many masterpieces in all areas of the arts - painting, music, literature and the cinema. Italian museums are full of Etruscan art and pieces from the Magna Graecia period and there are many examples of early Christian art such as the beautiful mosaics in Ravenna *(left)*.

ART

Italy's wealth of art really began in the 11th and 12th centuries with the rise of Romanesque art and individual artists such as Nicola Pisano (1225-1278).

Giotto (di Bondone, 1266/7-1337), the greatest genius of the Italian Gothic period came from Tuscany. He introduced fresco cycles - telling the story of a saint or prophet in the form of pictures. His greatest achievement is the St. Francis cycle at Basilica di St. Francesco in Assisi.

The Renaissance was Italy's most spectacular artistic period. Famous artists of that time include Sandro Botticelli (1444-1510), Fra Filippo Lippi (1406-1469), Titian (Tiziano Vecellio, 1477-1576), Raphael (Raffaello Sanzio 1483-1520) and Donatello (Donato de' Bardi, 1368-1466) to name but a few.

LEONARDO DA VINCI (1452-1519)

Leonardo da Vinci painted many masterpieces such as the *Mona Lisa* and *The Last Supper*. His anatomical drawings and interest in science made him a true Renaissance figure. He invented many things including a flying machine.

MICHAELANGELO BUONARROTI (1475-1564)

Michaelangelo painted the Sistine Chapel in Rome and is also famous for the sculptures of David and the Pietà, carved from Carrara marble.

MUSIC

Music is another great Italian tradition. One of the most famous Italian composers is Antonio Vivaldi (1675-1741) who composed *The Four Seasons*.
  Italy is the home of popular opera and some of the most famous operas in the world were composed by Italians.

GIUSEPPE VERDI (1813-1901)

Il Trovatore and *Rigoletto* (composed between 1851 and 1853) made Verdi famous in Italy. He later achieved world recognition with his later works such as *Aida* (1871), *Otello* (1887) and *Falstaff* (1893).

GIACOMO PUCCINI (1858-1924)

The works of Puccini include *La Bohème, Tosca, Madame Butterfly* and *Turandot*.

GIOACCHINO ROSSINI (1792-1868)

Rossini is famous for operas such as *The Barber of Seville* and *William Tell*.

Italy is also famous for its great singers including the tenors Enrico Caruso (1873-1921), Luciano Pavarotti, who is perhaps best known for his global appearances with "The Three Tenors", and Andrea Bocelli.

LITERATURE

Famous Italian writers include the poet Dante Alighieri (1265-1321) who wrote *The Divine Comedy.* Other renowned medieval writers were Francesco Petrarch (1304-1374), Giovanni Boccaccio (1313-75) who wrote the *Decameron* - ten witty stories - and Machiavelli, author of *The Prince* - a book about political theory. A famous author of today is Umberto Eco who wrote *The Name of the Rose*, a medieval whoddunit.

THEATRE

Italian theatre flourished in the 18th century with the Commedia dell'Arte and the comic plays of the Venetian playwright Carlo Goldoni. The famous characters of the Commedia dell'Arte are *Pantalone, Dottore Graziano, Brighella* and *Arlecchino* (Harlequin *[below]*). They usually wore masks and each character spoke his own dialect. Plays spoken in dialect are still popular.

A recent successful film from Italy has been *Life Is Beautiful* (1997).

CINEMA

Modern cinema is another great part of Italy's artistic heritage with film directors such as Roberto Rossellini, Federico Fellini , Franco Zeffirelli and Bernardo Bertolucci.

Say it in Italian:
la musica - music
l'artista - artist
il dipinto - painting
il libro - book
il teatro - theatre
il film - film

Holidays and Festivals

Italy has 10 national holidays a year. Whenever one falls on a Thursday or a Tuesday, Italians usually take the Friday or Monday as holiday as well. On these national holidays, banks, public offices, most shops and some museums and galleries are closed

Italians love festivals and local feast days are held in honour of each town's patron saint. There is usually a procession where a statue of the saint is carried around the town or village.

The traditional Pope's blessing is held every Easter Sunday in the Vatican, and in July the *Noiantri* (we others) festival is held in Trastevere, the old quarter of Rome. This is a street festival of music and fireworks by the river Tiber.

There are many festivals around 15 August and this is the time when Italians take their main holiday. Shops can be closed for the whole month.

The week before Ash Wednesday is known as *Carnevale* (goodbye to meat) or Carnival. People all over Italy wear fancy dress and there are processions and funfairs. The Carnival in Venice is very famous and everyone dresses up in masks and 18th century costume. There is a procession of gondolas along the Grand Canal and many masked balls are held.

In Florence on Easter Sunday morning, the *Scoppio del Carro* takes place in front of the cathedral. A highly decorated cart is filled with fireworks which are lit when a mechanical dove is freed from the altar of the cathedral. This festival commemorates the day on which knights returned to Florence after the First Crusade.

The *Palio* in Siena is a horse race held on 2 July and 15 August each year. People from different quarters dress in 15th century costume and form a procession to the main square. There is a display of flag-throwing and bareback horse riders from 10 of the quarters race around the square at breakneck speed. The winner gets a huge painted silk flag - the Palio.

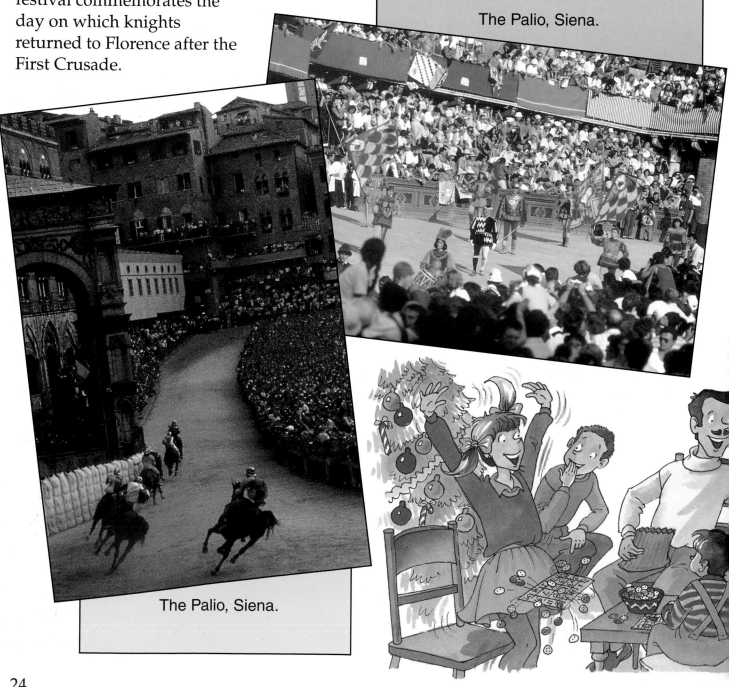

The Palio, Siena.

The Palio, Siena.

Christmas celebrations start on 24 December with a big evening meal and Midnight Mass. Presents are exchanged both on Christmas Day and on 6 January, the Epiphany. Tombola is a game played by many families during the Christmas period. It can be played by any number of players and a caller.

YOU WILL NEED:

1 piece of cardboard and pencil per player

ruler

a couple of sheets of paper

paper bag

counters, buttons, or similar

scissors

To make the game

1. Rule 20 small squares onto each player's piece of card. Write a number from 1-50 in each square.

2. Draw 50 squares, the same size as the ones you have just drawn, onto a piece of paper. Number them from 1 to 50, cut them out and put them in the paper bag.

To play the game

The caller picks the squares out of the bag, one at a time, and calls out the numbers. Players then cover any numbers that they have on their cards. The first player to cover a complete card calls out "Tombola" and is the winner.

In Naples on New Year's Day, fireworks are lit and people throw old things out of the windows. All the ships in the harbour sound their horns.

In the wine producing areas, there is always a celebration at harvest time in the autumn. There are fairs and dancing when the new wine is tasted.

Say it in Italian:
le ferie - holidays
la festa - festival
il Natale - Christmas
la Pasqua - Easter
il compleanno - birthday
l'onomastico - saint's day

Mystery Masks

To disguise yourself for a Venetian Carnival ...

YOU WILL NEED:

a wipeable surface to work on

2 small sheets of newspaper (torn into little strips)

petroleum jelly

modeling clay

fungicide-free wallpaper paste

small kitchen knife

sandpaper

pointed scissors

modeling tool

white acrylic paint

paint brushes

water-based paints

clear household varnish

braid

glue

garden stick

sequins etc to decorate

To make the plasticine mould

1. Knead the plasticine with your hands to warm it. Roll some of it into thick "sausages" and use these to form the outline of a half-face mask.

2. Fill in the outline with lumps of plasticine to made a flat-topped shape.

3. Hold the plasticine mould against your face and carefully mark the position of your eyes.

4. Cut holes for your eyes with the knife. Smooth the edges of these holes with the modelling tool.

5. Add small lumps of plasticine to make a nose. Blend the nose into the mould with the modelling tool.

To make the papier mâché mask

6. Cover the surface of the plasticine mould with petroleum jelly. Dip some of the newspaper strips into the wallpaper paste and cover the mould with a layer of paper. Wait for the glued paper to dry and add another layer. Your mask will need about six layers in total.

7. When your mask is completely dry, ease it away from the mould.

8. Gently rub your mask with sandpaper to smooth it, and neaten the edges with the scissors.

9. Paint your mask with a coat of white acrylic paint. This will help strengthen the papier mâché and leave you with a good surface for painting.

10. Once the acrylic paint has dried, you can paint your mask any colour you like. To give your colours a shiny finish, add a coat of clear varnish once the paint has dried.

11. To decorate your mask, glue braid, sequins or other trimmings onto the front of your mask.

12. Ask an adult to carefully pierce a small hole in the bottom rim of the mask. Paint the garden stick, push it through the hole and glue it to the back of your mask.

Italian History

Italy is an old country with a lot of history. Here are just a few key events and people.

THE ETRUSCANS

Nobody is sure where the Etruscans came from, but between 700 and 500 BC they ruled in Tuscany, north to the Po Valley, and south towards Naples. Their society was highly organised and evidence can be seen of their tombs, gold and metal ornaments, buildings, roads, canals and sewers.

MAGNA-GRAECIA

The Etruscans were influenced by the Greeks who, arriving in the 8th century BC, set up colonies in Sicily, Naples, Paestum and Taranto. The Greek mathematician, Pythagoras, invented his famous theory in Calabria.

ROME

According to legend, Rome was founded by Romulus in 753 BC. Romulus and his twin-brother Remus were abandoned by their mother and suckled by a she-wolf. This is Rome's symbol. Rome broke free from Etruscan rule in 510 BC and established a republic which lasted five centuries.

Julius Caesar ended the Republic by becoming a dictator. He was assasinated on the Ides of March (14th) 44 BC. His adopted son, Augustus, established the Roman Empire in 30 BC. The invasion by Attila the Hun and the sacking of Rome by the Goths and Vandals brought an end to the Roman empire in Italy.

CHARLEMAGNE

In 800, Charlemagne had conquered Italy and was crowned by the Pope as Emperor in Rome.

MARCO POLO

Marco Polo (1254-1324), from Venice, sailed to the Orient and brought back many treasures.

CITY STATES

Rivalry became stronger than ever in the 12th century and Italy as a whole became impossible to rule. Independent communes became city states. These included Venice, Genoa, Florence and Milan, ruled by the *Visconti* family.

GALILEO GALILEI (1564-1642)

Galileo was a great mathematician and inventor of the telescope. He was hounded by the church for saying that the Earth was round and one of many planets in orbit around the Sun.

VIVA VERDI!

In the 19th century, there was a great struggle for the unification of all the separate Italian states. It was led by Giuseppe Mazzini, Giuseppe Garibaldi and Count Camillo di Cavour. Public meetings were banned and the opera house became one of the few places where large numbers of Italians could gather legally.

Verdi's operas were famous for their patriotic messages and as more patriots began to look to the king as a future leader of a united Italy, Verdi's name took on new significance. By shouting their approval of the composer, they could also send a coded message of defiance - V.E.R.D.I! - Vittorio Emanuele, Re D'Italia!

TIME BAND

9th c. BC Etruscans settle in Italy
8th c. BC Greeks in Sicily and the South
510 BC Roman Republic established
49-44 BC Julius Caesar rules as dictator
79 AD Pompeii and Herculaneum are destroyed by the eruption of Vesuvius
800 Charlemagne crowned Emperor in Rome
1860 Garibaldi's Expedition of a Thousand
1861 Kingdom of Italy formed
1871 Rome made capital of unified Italy
1915 Italy joins British, French and Russians in World War I
1921 Italian Communist Party founded
1929 A separate Vatican State is established
1940 Italy joins Germany in World War II
1949 Italy becomes a member of NATO
1957 Italy joins EEC which becomes the European Union in 1993
2002 Italy adopts the Euro as its currency

MUSSOLINI AND FASCISM

In the depression after World War I, Benito Mussolini (1883-1945) founded the Fascist party in 1921. He marched on Rome as leader *(Il Duce)* of the Fascists and formed a government in 1922.

Mussolini supported Hitler in World War II. After the American liberation in 1943, he fell from power and was executed in 1945.

Say it in Italian:
la storia - history
il re - king
il soldato - soldier
il presidente - president
la politica - politics

Picture Pairs

Play Picture Pairs and see how many of the Italian words in this book you actually remember! The instructions given here are for two to four players, but as your Italian vocabulary increases, you might like to make more cards and include more players.

YOU WILL NEED:

OLD MAGAZINES

WRAPPING PAPER

METAL RULER

GLUE

SCISSORS

STIFF PAPER

THICK CARD

CUTTING BOARD

PAINTS OR CRAYONS

PENCIL

CRAFT KNIFE

To make the cards

1. Draw 50 rectangles of the same size onto the card and carefully cut them out using the craft knife.

2. Draw another 50 rectangles onto the wrapping paper and cut them out too. These rectangles should be about 2 cm longer and wider than the card ones.

3. Cut the the corners of the paper rectangles as shown and glue them onto your cards.

4. Draw 25 rectangles, slightly smaller than your cards onto the stiff paper and cut them out.

5. Choose 25 Italian words from this book and write them down with their English translations. (Keep this list beside you when you play the game.)

6. Look through the magazines and cut out any photographs which illustrate the words you have chosen. If you can't find suitable pictures, cut out some more rectangles from stiff paper and paint pictures of your words on them.

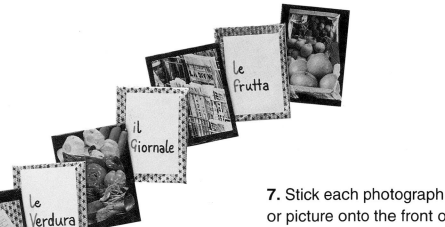

7. Stick each photograph or picture onto the front of one of your cards. Glue the stiff paper rectangles onto the rest of the pack and write a Italian word from your list on each one.

To play the game
The object of Picture Pairs is to collect pairs of cards made up of words and their matching picture.

Each player starts the game with seven cards. The rest of the pack is placed face down on the table. If you have any pairs, put them on the table in front of you.

Then ask one of the other players if he/she has a card that you need to make a pair. If that player has the card requested, he/she must hand it over and you win the pair and have another turn. If he/she does not have the card, you take a card from the pack in the middle and the turn passes to the next person.

All word cards must be translated into English. If you can not remember the translation of the word, look it up and miss your next go.

The player who pairs all his cards first is the winner.

Index

architecture 7
artists 20
arts 20, 21

Basilica 8

Capri 18
card games 19
Carnival 23
cars 5, 16
Charlemagne 28
Christmas 24
cinema 22
climate 6
Coliseum 7
Commedia dell' Arte 22
composers 21
currency 5

da Vinci, Leonardo 20
design 17
dialects 6

Etruscans 28

fashion 17
festivals 23
flag 4
Florence 8
food 10, 11

Galilei, Galileo 29
geography 6
government 5

Harlequin 22
history 28, 29
holidays 23
housing 14

ice cream 11
industry 15, 16, 17
Ischia 18

lakes 18
Leaning Tower of Pisa
leather 17
literature 22

Mafia 5
magazines 15
Magna-Graecia 28
marble 16
Marco Polo 28
Michaelangelo 20
music 21
Mussolini 29

national anthem 4
newspapers 15
New Year's Day 25

opera 21

Palio 24
pasta 11
pizza 11, 12-13
police 15
Pompeii 7

Ponte Vecchio 8
Pope 6, 14, 23
Pythagoras 28

Ravenna 20
religion 14
Renaissance 20
Romulus and Remus 28

San Marino 6
school 14
shopping 10, 23
Sicily 18
Siena 24
sport 18, 19
steel 16

technology 16, 17
television 15
theatre 22
Tiramisù 11
tombola 25
tourism 18
transport 17

Vatican City 6, 8, 23
Venice 8, 17
Verdi, Giuseppe 21, 29
volcanoes 7

writers 22